THE ANGLO-SAXONS

Written by
Rowena Loverance

Illustrated by
David Price and Tracy Fennell

Edited by
Caroline White

Designed by
Jo Digby

Picture research by
Helen Taylor

Contents

The march of time

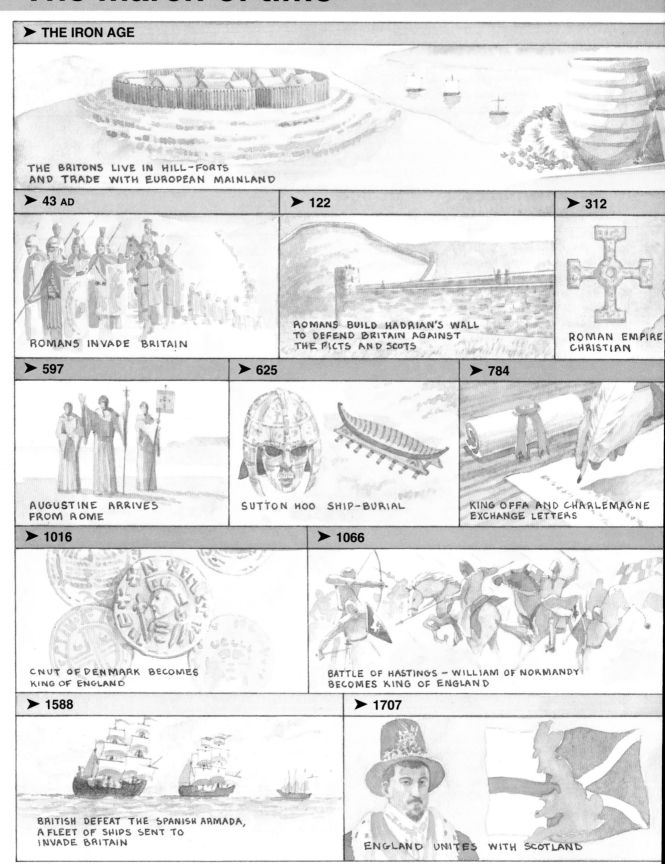

➤ **THE IRON AGE**

THE BRITONS LIVE IN HILL-FORTS
AND TRADE WITH EUROPEAN MAINLAND

➤ **43 AD**

ROMANS INVADE BRITAIN

➤ **122**

ROMANS BUILD HADRIAN'S WALL
TO DEFEND BRITAIN AGAINST
THE PICTS AND SCOTS

➤ **312**

ROMAN EMPIRE
CHRISTIAN

➤ **597**

AUGUSTINE ARRIVES
FROM ROME

➤ **625**

SUTTON HOO SHIP-BURIAL

➤ **784**

KING OFFA AND CHARLEMAGNE
EXCHANGE LETTERS

➤ **1016**

CNUT OF DENMARK BECOMES
KING OF ENGLAND

➤ **1066**

BATTLE OF HASTINGS - WILLIAM OF NORMANDY
BECOMES KING OF ENGLAND

➤ **1588**

BRITISH DEFEAT THE SPANISH ARMADA,
A FLEET OF SHIPS SENT TO
INVADE BRITAIN

➤ **1707**

ENGLAND UNITES WITH SCOTLAND

➤ 55 BC

ROMAN GENERAL JULIUS CAESAR ARRIVES IN BRITAIN

➤ 406

ROMAN ARMIES LEAVE BRITAIN
ANGLO-SAXONS BEGIN
TO ARRIVE

➤ 500

KING ARTHUR MAY HAVE
FOUGHT THE ANGLO-SAXONS

793

VIKINGS BEGIN TO RAID
BRITAIN

➤ 878

KING ALFRED DEFEATS
THE VIKINGS

➤ 973

EDGAR IS CROWNED KING
OF ALL ENGLAND

1215

MAGNA CARTA — KING JOHN IS FORCED
TO WRITE DOWN LAWS

➤ 1485

HENRY VII BECOMES FIRST TUDOR KING

1815

BATTLE OF WATERLOO
ENDS WARS WITH FRANCE

➤ 1973

BRITAIN JOINS THE COMMON MARKET

Who were the Anglo-Saxons?

The Anglo-Saxons first appear in history as different groups of people living along the north coast of the European mainland. There weren't just the Angles and the Saxons – there were the Jutes and the Frisians and many other groups. We call all these people who left their homes to settle in England 'Anglo-Saxons'.

What did they look like?

Most Anglo-Saxon bodies survive only as skeletons. This man, however, was found in a peat bog in Denmark, where some of the Anglo-Saxons came from. His skin has been preserved by the peat, so we can get a good idea of what the early Anglo-Saxons looked like.

Why did they settle in England?

The coast of the European mainland where these people lived was often flooded by the sea. Villages were built on large mounds of earth to protect them from the floods, but there became less and less room on the mounds as time went by. They could not build upwards, as in cities today, so they had to look for land elsewhere. The obvious place was across the North Sea – in Britain.

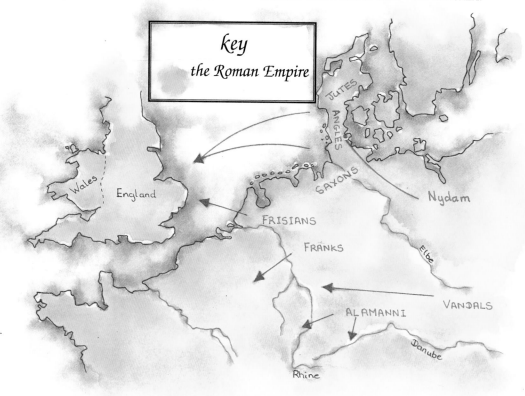

key
the Roman Empire

JUTES

ANGLES

Wales

England

SAXONS

Nydam

FRISIANS

FRANKS

Elbe

VANDALS

ALAMANNI

Danube

Rhine

Radio-carbon dating

How do we know that the man, the ship and the prow all date back to Anglo-Saxon times?

All living things take in radioactive carbon (C14) from the atmosphere. When they die, the radioactive carbon begins to decay. Scientists know the rate at which it decays and can also measure how much is left in a dead plant or animal. They are therefore able to work out how long ago the plant or animal died.

Ships

The Angles, Saxons and other groups sailed across to Britain in ships like the one below, which was found in a peat bog at Nydam in Denmark. They were like huge rowing boats with a large steering oar. The prow at the front may have been carved to make the ship appear very threatening. This prow was found in a river in Belgium.

The Anglo-Saxons in Britain

In the year 400, Britain must have looked like a strong province of the Roman Empire, with people in the South living in Roman towns or in fine country houses with central heating and mosaic floors.

But the Roman Empire itself was growing weaker. Forts had to be built by the sea to defend Britain against the Anglo-Saxon raiders, who came looking for gold and silver to carry home with them. You can see the nine Roman forts in this picture.

In 406, the Roman army left Britain to fight enemies closer to home, so Britain now had to look after itself.

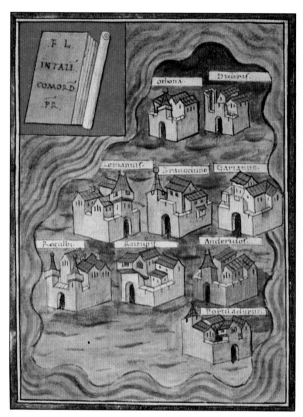

Things changed for the people who remained, the 'Celts' and 'Britons'. As the towns were gradually deserted, life became more like it had been before the Romans arrived.

Soldiers

We are not sure when or how the first Anglo-Saxons arrived in Britain. Some may have been paid to fight for the Roman army. This Anglo-Saxon soldier was buried in full uniform near Dorchester-on-Thames in Oxfordshire. A woman's grave was found next to his, so he had probably married a local woman. This could explain why some Anglo-Saxons have British names: they are of mixed race.

6

Hengist and Horsa

The Anglo-Saxons wrote a book called the *Anglo-Saxon Chronicle* which tells us about England in their times. It begins with the story of Hengist and Horsa being invited over to Britain in the year 449 to help fight the Picts and the Scots. These tribes lived in Scotland and were attacking the North of England. Instead of returning home afterwards, Hengist and Horsa are said to have turned against the king of the Britons and taken his kingdom from him. We do not know if this story is true or not, but more and more Anglo-Saxons began to settle in England after that time.

War and peace

Much of the settlement may have been peaceful, but the *Anglo-Saxon Chronicle* tells us of some dreadful battles. In the year 491, a Saxon king called AElle attacked the Roman fort at Pevensey in East Sussex. The Saxons killed all the people in the fort, until 'there was not even one Briton left'.

The Roman fort at Pevensey

Changing languages

Latin, the language of the Roman Empire, almost completely disappeared in Anglo-Saxon England. However, there are still some Latin place-names left in England today:

camp	= plain
caster	= fort
eccles	= church
port	= harbour
wic (vicus)	= town

Can you find any of these on a map of where you live?

Was there ever a King Arthur?

King Arthur is thought to have been a British war-leader who held off the Anglo-Saxon raiders at the beginning of the sixth century. It is said that his group of knights sat at a Round Table and had many adventures together. The group, however, broke up when Arthur's wife, Queen Guinevere, fell in love with his best friend, Sir Lancelot.

Are these stories true? Did King Arthur ever really exist? Look at the evidence on these two pages and try to decide for yourself.

Written evidence

We can learn a lot about Anglo-Saxon times from books which survive today. Many of these books talk about 'Arthur' but were written much later than the sixth century. This evidence is therefore not very reliable.

> From that time forth sometimes the Britons, and sometimes the enemy, were victorious, up to the year of the siege of Mount Badon, which was almost the most recent but not the least slaughter of these gallow-birds.

A Welsh monk called Gildas wrote this in the sixth century. Arthur is thought to have led the Britons at the Battle of Mount Badon, but Gildas does not mention him by name.

> Then Arthur fought against those men in those days with the kings of the Britons, but he was leader of battles. [There follows a list of twelve battles, of which Mount Badon is the last.] And in all the battles he was victor.

Nennius, another Welsh monk, calls Arthur a 'leader of battles'. He wrote this in the tenth century.

> 518: Battle of Badon in which Arthur carried the Cross of Our Lord Jesus Christ on his shoulders for three days and three nights and the Britons were victors.

This comes from the *Annals of Wales*, a list of dates in Welsh history. The list was not put together until the eleventh century.

Archaeological evidence

An archaeologist is someone who finds out about the past by looking at things buried under the ground.

Remains of an ancient hill-fort at Cadbury in Somerset could be where Arthur and his army lived. Archaeologists have found pottery and the remains of wooden walls which show that people were living there in the sixth century.

Archaeologists think the hall at Cadbury would have looked like this.

What the stories say

Arthur was born at Tintagel in Cornwall.

Could this Round Table, which hangs in Winchester Castle, be the one Arthur and his knights sat round?

A cross was found over King Arthur's grave at Glastonbury.

Villages

Anglo-Saxon houses were built of wood and so have rotted away over the years. However, we can still find out what the villages looked like, and learn about the Anglo-Saxon way of life, by looking at clues buried under the ground.

West Stow

By carefully digging up the earth, archaeologists have uncovered, or excavated, an Anglo-Saxon village at West Stow in Suffolk. The houses have been rebuilt to show us what the village would have looked like in Anglo-Saxon times. Most villages were made up of only three or four farms.

Seeds found beneath the ground tell us that wheat, rye and barley were grown. Animal bones show that sheep, cattle, pigs, small horses, hens and geese were kept, as well as cats and dogs. Bones of perch and pike have also been found: the people of West Stow must have eaten lots of fish from the river.

Houses

The Anglo-Saxons built two types of house. One had wooden posts set in a rectangle about 10 metres long. The holes where the posts went into the ground can still be found today.

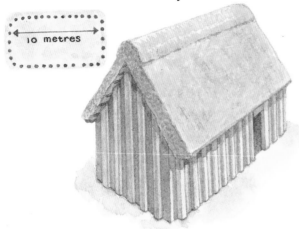

The other type of house had just a few posts at either end of a large hole. Did the Anglo-Saxons live in holes in the ground? A wooden floor was probably laid across the hole, so it would not touch the soil and rot with damp.

Photographs from the air

How do we know where to look for the site of an Anglo-Saxon village?

One way is by taking a photograph from the air. The old ditches, pits and walls of the villages are still buried beneath the ground. Crops grow better over the ditches and pits than over the walls, where the soil is not as deep. The patterns made by the crops can be seen from the air.

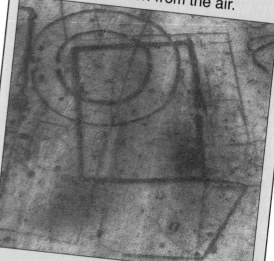

This photograph was taken from an aeroplane. It shows the Anglo-Saxon village at Mucking in Essex. Each small, dark dot is the dug-out floor of an Anglo-Saxon house or workshop.

Everyday things

Most of the things which people needed were made in the village. Iron knives, bone combs and pottery were all made here. These combs were found at West Stow. Can you see the patterns on them?

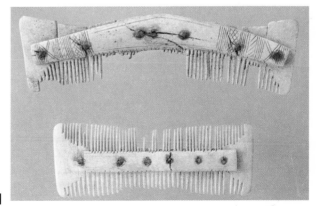

11

People

We can learn a lot about Anglo-Saxon people by looking at their graves. They could be either buried or cremated, but in each case the dead person was accompanied by the possessions he or she would need in the next life.

Cremation

The burnt remains of a person's bones and personal possessions, such as beads and combs, were collected and placed in a small pot. Sometimes more than one body would go into a pot.

Whole cemeteries full of cremation pots have been found. At Spong Hill in Suffolk, the cemetery contained over 2000 pots and was in use for some 200 years. This means that about ten people were buried there each year. Perhaps it was the cemetery for several villages.

A cremation pot from Loveden Hill in Lincolnshire

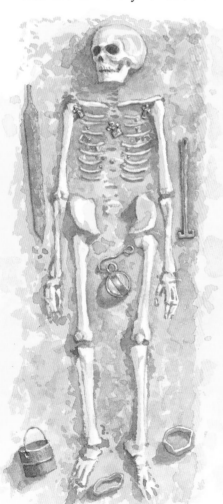

Burial

Graves where the bodies were buried give us a good idea of what the Anglo-Saxons looked like. We can tell that women from different parts of the country wore different styles of dress and jewellery. This woman was an Angle and fastened her dress with long brooches. Saxon women used round, saucer-shaped brooches.

Puzzle pieces

Archaeologists have puzzled over these objects which are often found in Anglo-Saxon women's graves. What do you think they are? The answers are on page 48.

iron

rock-crystal in a bronze ring

bronze

The answers are on page 48.

(see pages 18–19)

Evidence from human bones

Scientists who study bones have found that half the Anglo-Saxons died by the age of 25 and very few lived beyond the age of 40.

They have also found that some did not die a natural death. At Sutton Hoo in Suffolk (see pages 18–19) bodies have been found without a head or with their limbs in impossible positions. These Anglo-Saxons had probably been sacrificed when the king was buried there.

You can tell how wealthy a man was by looking at the weapons he was buried with. Someone buried with a sword was better off than this man, whose main weapon was his spear.

Gods and religion

The Anglo-Saxons looked to their gods to protect them in this world, and to welcome them to the next world after their death. The chief of the gods was Woden. He was married to Frig, the goddess who made things grow. Thunor was the god of sky and thunder. Tiw was the god of war.

Power of the gods

The power of the pagan gods was often shown through animals. Boars with sharp tusks were used to decorate helmets. A warrior wearing a helmet like this would hope to frighten his enemy.

This Anglo-Saxon buckle is decorated with a snake pattern. The snake represented cunning, a quality which the Anglo-Saxons admired in their gods. Woden was especially cunning – he was a master of disguises.

Fierce birds with tearing claws had the same sort of power. This shield has been made to look like a raven, a bird which often accompanied Woden in Anglo-Saxon folk-tales. The raven was thought to haunt the battlefield and was called 'chooser of the slain'.

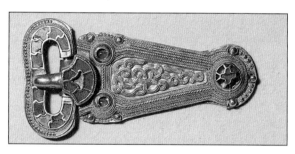

Pagan worship

We do not know what the Anglo-Saxons thought their gods looked like. Nor do we know how they practised their religion. Our only written evidence comes from Christian writers, who wanted to destroy the old pagan beliefs and practices. They say that animals were sacrificed in temples to statues of gods in human form. The man on this buckle is wearing a helmet engraved with bird's heads. He may be taking part in the worship of Woden.

Pagan priests

Coifi was a High Priest who gave up his pagan beliefs once Christianity had been brought to England. Pagan priests were not allowed to carry weapons or ride anything more lively than a mare. But Coifi borrowed the king's stallion and rode up to the temple, while the crowd watched to see if he would fall off. He threw a spear at the pagan statues and demanded that the temple be burnt down. The *Anglo-Saxon Chronicle* tells us that all this happened at a place called Goodmanham, not far from York.

Names and places

Lots of place-names in England still use the names of Anglo-Saxon gods:

Tysoe	= Tiw's spur
Wednesbury	= Woden's fort
Thunderfield	= Thor's plain
Freefolk	= Frig's people

The Anglo-Saxon gods also gave their names to four of our days of the week. Can you see which ones?

Traces of our pagan past

A boar's head is sometimes cooked at Christmas by people today.

The three women on this whalebone box could control the future. They turn up today in Shakespeare's play *Macbeth*.

15

Christianity

Christianity reached Britain during Roman times but slowly disappeared when the Anglo-Saxons arrived.

However, it did survive in Cornwall, Scotland and Wales, where the Anglo-Saxons did not settle.

The Roman Church

It was Pope Gregory, the head of the Christian Church, who sent some missionaries from Rome to England to convert the Anglo-Saxons to Christianity. They were led by a man called Augustine. The missionaries had only gone a short way before they wanted to turn back. After all, they did not want to go to a 'barbarous, fierce and pagan nation, of whose very language they were ignorant'.

Augustine eventually arrived in Kent in the year 597. King AEthelbert of Kent met him in the open air, believing this would protect him from any magic. Soon AEthelbert and many of his people had become Christians. An abbey was built at Canterbury and Augustine became the first Archbishop of Canterbury, working to spread the new Christian faith throughout the country.

The Celtic Church

A British monk called Patrick had brought Christianity to the Celts in Ireland in the fifth century. Thirty years before Augustine arrived in England, a monk called Columba sailed from Ireland to the small island of Iona, just off the coast of Scotland, and built a monastery there. This stone cross, decorated with circles and spirals, is from the monastery on Iona. People would gather round it to pray.

The monks then sailed to the island of Lindisfarne, just off the coast of Northumbria, and built a monastery there. Monks from Lindisfarne went all over Northumbria telling people about Jesus. They were greatly admired and loved.

Animals were also fond of these saintly monks. One story tells us that a monk called Cuthbert spent all night singing psalms in the sea. In the morning, two sea otters came and dried his feet with their fur!

Churches

Churches began to be built throughout the country. Most were made of wood, but some were built in stone. This stone church, at Bradwell-on-Sea in Essex, is still used by Christians today.

Sutton Hoo

More than twenty great mounds of earth overlooking the River Deben in Suffolk mark the site of Sutton Hoo. In 1939, archaeologists opened the largest mound and found traces of an Anglo-Saxon ship, and in it a wealth of possessions. This was the grave of a very rich person. It was the most spectacular Anglo-Saxon discovery ever made in England.

Who was buried there?

The body itself was never found. The sand at Sutton Hoo is very acidic and must have destroyed all traces of it. However, the objects buried in the ship, such as these gold fastenings, suggest it was the grave of a king – probably the king of East Anglia, the Anglo-Saxon kingdom in which Sutton Hoo lies. The fastenings would have been worn on the king's shoulders to hold together his leather coat of armour.

The site of the king's palace has yet to be found, but this bronze cauldron must have hung in a high hall and could have fed a large number of people.

Whetstone and standard

Objects like this whetstone and iron standard have not been found anywhere else. The whetstone (a shaped stone for sharpening swords) is unusual because it has never been used to sharpen anything. Perhaps it was carried as a sign of royal power. The enormous standard would have been carried in front of the king in battle.

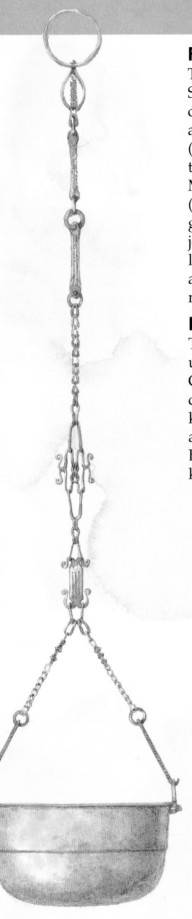

Faraway places

There were objects in the grave from Sweden, where some Anglo-Saxons came from, but also from Gaul (France) and the eastern Mediterranean (Turkey). The garnets in this jewelled purse lid came from as far away as Afghanistan. The king must have traded with many countries.

Pagan or Christian?

The king does not appear to have made up his mind between the pagan gods and Christianity. A ship-burial was a pagan custom, but these spoons suggest he knew something of the new religion: they are both engraved with names from the Bible. They could have been given to the king as a present when he was baptised.

New finds at Sutton Hoo

Archaeologists are still working at Sutton Hoo. They have recently found the body of a young man under one of the other mounds of earth. He had been buried with his horse and its harness. The rest of the graves, however, have had their contents stolen by grave robbers.

Beowulf

Beowulf is a long Anglo-Saxon poem about the adventures of a hero called Beowulf. Part of the poem, written below, describes a ship-burial in Denmark, where some Anglo-Saxons came from. It is the funeral of Scyld Shefing, great-grandfather of Hrothgar, King of the Danes. In what ways is it like the ship-burial at Sutton Hoo? How is it different?

> 'A boat with a ringed neck rode in the haven...
> and there they laid out their lord and master,
> dealer of wound gold, in the waist of the ship,
> in majesty by the mast.
>
> A mound of treasures from far countries was fetched aboard her, and it is said that no boat was ever more bravely fitted out with the weapons of a warrior...
>
> High over head they hoisted and fixed
> a gold standard; gave him to the flood,
> let the seas take him...'

The poem goes on to tell us about Grendel, a terrible monster who comes from the dark places of the earth. One night, while Hrothgar and his followers are asleep, Grendel comes to their hall and seizes 30 warriors. He comes again the next night, and the next, until the hall stands empty. Grendel continues to terrorize Hrothgar's hall for twelve years.

Meanwhile, across the sea in Sweden, Beowulf hears of Hrothgar's troubles and sails to his hall. That night the monster appears again. He rips one warrior apart and swallows him – feet, hands and all. Beowulf grabs Grendel with his bare hands and the hall trembles as they struggle. At last the monster tears himself away, but he has left his arm in Beowulf's grip. The hero hangs the arm up as a trophy.

Beowulf's trials are not yet over, for Grendel's mother comes to take revenge. She too is a dreadful monster, who lives at the bottom of a deep lake. Beowulf wrestles with her beneath the water until he manages to drive a sword through her neck. As he rises to the surface, where his friends are anxiously waiting, the waters of the lake are mixed with blood.

Beowulf's last fight is back home in Sweden against a fire-breathing dragon. Beowulf dies in the fight, but first he manages to gain the dragon's hoard of treasure. The poem ends with Beowulf's own funeral fire and the raising of a great earth mound to his memory.

Manuscripts

There are many books which retell the story of *Beowulf* but they are all taken from just one hand-written version, or manuscript, which was written in about the year 1000. The manuscript was badly damaged in a fire in 1731. If it had not survived, we would not know the story of *Beowulf* at all.

Bards

The story of *Beowulf* takes place in Denmark and Sweden, before the Anglo-Saxons settled in England. It would have been passed down over the years by bards, or story-tellers, to the sound of the harp. You can see a bard playing a small harp in this picture.

The poem was probably written down for the first time when the Anglo-Saxons became Christians, because the new religion is often referred to.

Runes and riddles

At first, the Anglo-Saxons wrote using letters called 'runes'. Here is their alphabet. Underneath are the letters we use today.

ᚠᚢᚦᚩᚱᚳᚷᚹᚻᚾᛁᛄᛈ

f u th o r k g w h n i j h p

The runic alphabet is called the 'futhork'. Can you see why?

ᛉᛋᛏᛒᛖᛗᛚᛝᛞᛟᚪᚫᚣᛠ

x s t b e m l ng d œ a æ y ea

The Anglo-Saxons believed these runes had magical powers. This may be why they carved them on rings, which they wore to keep away sickness and danger. They also wrote them on cremation pots.

Sometimes they made up a pattern of runes, as we might say 'abracadabra'. Sometimes they wrote out the whole futhork. Perhaps this was a kind of magic too.

When the Anglo-Saxons became Christians and started to use the Roman alphabet, they often treated the letters in the same magical way. The first half of the alphabet has been written on this ring...maybe there was another ring with the second half on it.

Riddles

Whether they were using runes or the Roman alphabet, the Anglo-Saxons loved to make up riddles. Can you solve the one below?

> ‘I hang,
> touching neither the sky
> nor the earth
> Growing hot from fires
> and sometimes bubbling
> like a whirlpool.’

The answer is a picture on page 19.

Anglo-Saxon riddles give a voice to something which does not usually speak. A famous Anglo-Saxon poem also uses this idea.

In the poem, the cross, or rood, on which Jesus was crucified is heard to speak:

> ‘I was reared up, a rood
> I raised the great King
> They pierced me with dark nails;
> the scars can still be clearly seen on
> me
> How they mocked at us both
> I was all moist with blood...’

Writing

Old English was the language of the Anglo-Saxons. English spoken today comes from the same language, although it has changed quite a lot over the years. Latin was the language of the Church. It was used to write religious books.

This page is from the *Anglo-Saxon Chronicle*, which was written in Old English using joined-up letters. The Anglo-Saxons used joined-up letters when they wanted to write something quickly. Printed letters were used to write important books to read aloud, such as the Bible.

Monasteries

Christianity is a religion which depends on a book: the Bible. The story of Jesus has been written down in the Bible so that everyone can read or listen to it. In an age before printing, the Bible and all other religious books had to be copied by hand. This copying took place in monasteries.

When the Anglo-Saxons became Christians, many men and women went into monasteries to become monks and nuns. They would spend most of their time praying to God, at night as well as during the day. The monasteries were often founded by the king and run by a member of his family.

The first monasteries were built of wood and had thatched roofs. But rich men like Benedict Biscop, who founded the monastery at Jarrow, had travelled abroad and seen buildings made of stone. So they brought builders across from Gaul to teach the Anglo-Saxons how to build in the 'Roman fashion'.

Besides spending time in prayer and copying religious books, the monks and nuns had all the other work of the monastery to see to. We know that Ceolfrith was a monastery baker before he became Abbot of Jarrow. His duties included sifting the flour, cleaning the oven and baking the bread.

The Lindisfarne Gospels

The *Lindisfarne Gospels* is one of the most famous books to survive from an Anglo-Saxon monastery. The book tells the story of the life of Jesus and has beautiful full-page illustrations and lots of decorated initial letters. It took the skin of at least 129 calves to make the parchment on which it is written, and all the writing and painting is the work of one man.

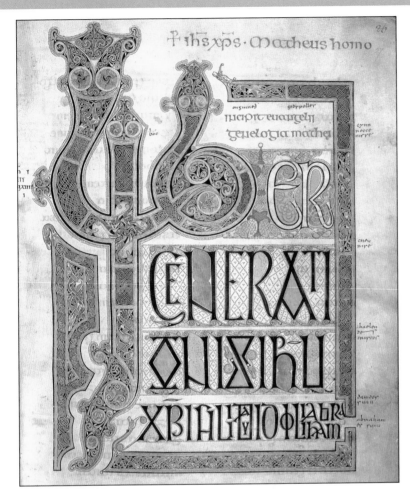

The first page from the Gospel according to Saint Matthew

Bede

The monks did not only copy books, they also wrote their own. A well-known Anglo-Saxon writer is Bede, a monk at the monastery at Jarrow. His most famous book is *A History of the English Church and People*, from which many of the stories in this book have been taken. He also wrote two books about Time, where he recommends dating years from the birth of Christ. This system is still used today.

School

The monasteries also served as the Anglo-Saxon schools. The basic lessons were reading, writing, singing and arithmetic. These led on to more advanced subjects, such as astronomy (the study of the stars), scripture (the study of the Bible) and computus (the calculation of time).

Children probably started school at the age of seven. Playing truant was not unheard of – the monks at Jarrow were warned to make sure that the boys did not spend their time hunting hares or digging foxes out of holes.

Women

Anglo-Saxon women were skilled in making everyday things such as clothes and pots. They were also important in the home, but they were not dependent on their husbands. Many chose not to marry at all.

Women were just as important as men in converting the Anglo-Saxons from their pagan beliefs to Christianity. King Edwin of Northumbria married a Christian called AEthelburga who helped to convert him to Christianity. Their daughter Eanfled was brought up to follow the customs of the Roman Church. Eanfled's husband, however, followed the customs of the Celtic Church. The two Churches had different ways of working out the date of Easter, and while her husband was celebrating Easter, Eanfled was still keeping the fast of Lent!

The meeting which resolved this problem, by deciding in favour of the Roman Church, was held at the monastery at Whitby. This monastery was run by a strong-minded woman called Hild. Bede tells us that both kings and ordinary people came to ask for Hild's advice, and that everyone who knew her called her 'mother'.

Nuns and their looks

Not all monasteries were as well run as Hild's. One book accuses some nuns of taking too much trouble over their looks:

> ❝They crimp the hair on their foreheads with a curling-iron. Instead of dark-grey veils on their heads, they wear brightly coloured head-dresses laced with ribbons hanging down as far as their ankles. They sharpen their finger-nails like falcons or hawks.❞

The nuns in this picture lived in Barking Abbey in Essex. Look at the decoration on some of their clothes. Do you think they have taken too much trouble over how they look?

Women's rights

The Anglo-Saxon laws which survive today make it clear that women had their own rights.

If a woman left her husband and took the children with her, she could take half the family's belongings. However, if she left the children with the father, she could not take as much.

If the father died, the mother was given six shillings to look after the child, as well as a cow in the summer and an ox in the winter. The kinsmen (male relatives) had to look after the home until the child had grown up.

A woman's influence

King Redwald of East Anglia came back from a stay in Kent announcing that he had become a Christian. His wife, however, persuaded him that this was a mistake. Redwald ended up putting a Christian altar at one end of his temple and a pagan altar for sacrifice at the other. If Redwald is the king who was buried at Sutton Hoo (see page 18), it would have been his wife who arranged for the great ship-burial.

Weaving

Anglo-Saxon women spun the wool from sheep into thread. They then wove the thread into cloth on a loom and used it to make clothes, covers and curtains. The pieces you can see here may have come from a cloth to put over a church altar. They are embroidered in gold thread and six colours of silk.

Kings and laws

When the Anglo-Saxons began to settle in England they lived in small tribal groups. These groups slowly developed into kingdoms, each with its own king and its own laws. Many of the kingdoms have given England its modern county names: Sussex, Essex and Middlesex are the kingdoms of the South, East and Middle Saxons.

Wergilds

Each Anglo-Saxon had a value in money. This was called a 'wergild'. A person of noble birth would have a high wergild, while a peasant would have a much lower one, and a slave would have an even lower one. This meant that if someone was killed or injured, the right amount of money could then be given to his or her family. However, a wergild did not have to be paid if a person caught stealing was killed.

The king was the most important person in the Anglo-Saxon kingdom and had the highest wergild. This helmet belonged to the king of East Anglia who was buried at Sutton Hoo. The picture on the cover of this book shows us what the helmet probably looked like when it was new.

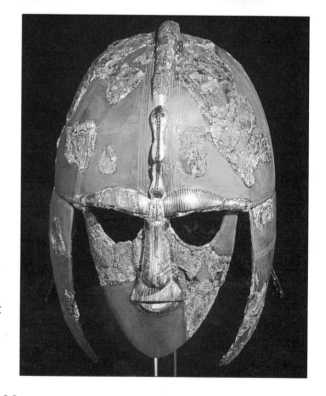

King Edwin

Today, people sometimes look back to the last century and think that things were better then. Bede says that in his time, the people of Northumbria looked back to the reign of King Edwin. It was said to be so peaceful during his reign that if a woman with a baby chose to wander across Northumbria from sea to sea, she could do so without danger.

King Edwin also saw to the needs of travellers in his kingdom. He ordered posts to be set up where there were clear springs of water beside a road. Bronze cups were hung here so that travellers could stop for a drink. These drinking posts were never vandalised because the people of Northumbria were afraid of King Edwin.

An eighth-century carving of a king can be seen on this stone from Repton in Derbyshire.

Royal palace at Yeavering

Archaeologists have discovered the site of a royal palace at Yeavering in Northumberland. They can tell from post-holes in the ground that there were several wooden halls, the largest over 24 metres long and 12 metres wide.

Traces of a large wooden grandstand have also been found at the site. The grandstand could hold about 300 people, or ten villages. King Edwin of Northumbria may have met here with his advisers.

Towns

Not everyone lived in villages or in the monasteries. Town life was very much a part of Anglo-Saxon England.

Roman towns

We used to think the Anglo-Saxons chose not to live in Roman towns. However, the remains of early Anglo-Saxon churches have now been found in Exeter, Leicester, London, St Albans and York.

Hamwic

The Anglo-Saxons began to build new towns in the late seventh century. Hamwic, known today as Southampton, was built along the River Itchen. It had a deep ditch all the way round to offer protection against attacks. The streets were laid out in a grid pattern, as with new towns built in Britain today. The wide main street probably held a weekly street market. There were no fences between the houses, which suggests that one person – the king – owned all the land in Hamwic.

Despite living close to the sea, the people of Hamwic did not eat much fish. Bones found buried beneath the ground show that they ate mainly beef, with some mutton and pork. They also ate lots of different cereals: wheat, barley, oats and peas. It was a well-balanced diet, even if we might find it rather dull.

Nearly every house in Hamwic made things to sell. Remains of metal, glass, bone and pottery have all been discovered either on the floor or in the backyard of the Anglo-Saxon houses. Large stones used for grinding corn have also been found, so each household probably ground its own corn.

Pottery

The Anglo-Saxons were skilled in making pots. They made them by hand until the seventh century, when they learnt to use the potter's wheel.

The town of Ipswich specialised in making pottery. Pots from here have been found all over East Anglia. The kilns where they were baked have also been discovered in a special area of the town.

Coins

Anglo-Saxon coins are often found buried with objects such as pots. Archaeologists can work out how old the coins are by looking at the writing and pictures on them, and this in turn can help to date the pots.

Up to 10 000 pennies could be made from one metal stamp, or die, before it wore out. Very few gold coins have been found. This may be because people took good care not to lose them. Silver coins, called 'sceattas', are far more common.

Missionaries and travel

The Anglo-Saxons never forgot their homeland. They traded with towns on the European mainland and missionaries were sent abroad to convert the Angles and Saxons from their pagan beliefs to Christianity.

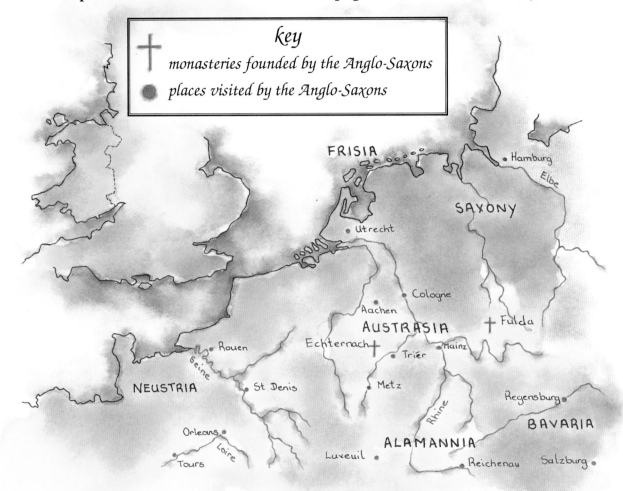

key

† monasteries founded by the Anglo-Saxons

● places visited by the Anglo-Saxons

FRISIA · Hamburg · Elbe

SAXONY

· Utrecht

· Cologne

Aachen

AUSTRASIA † Fulda

Echternach † · Trier · Mainz

· Rouen

Seine

· Metz

NEUSTRIA · St Denis

· Regensburg

Rhine

BAVARIA

Orleans ·

Loire ALAMANNIA

Luxeuil ·

· Tours · Reichenau Salzburg ·

Two well-known Anglo-Saxon missionaries are Boniface and Lul. Boniface travelled to Saxony (southern Germany) and Lul became Archbishop of Mainz. England's close links with the European mainland can be seen through the letters which they wrote and received. Anglo-Saxon books were certainly in demand – nearly every letter sent home to England asked for more copies of the book written by Bede.

Familiar news from home

❝During the past winter, the island of our race has been very savagely oppressed with cold and ice and with long and widespread storms of wind and rain, so that the hand of the scribe became sluggish and could not produce a very large number of books.❞

Cuthbert, Abbot of Monkwearmouth, to Lul in the dreadful winter of 764

Difficulties of being abroad

"My priests near the frontier of the pagans have a poor livelihood. They can get bread to eat, but cannot obtain clothing."

Boniface to Fulrad, Abbot of St Denys in Gaul (France)

The sound of home

"Send us a bell, as a great comfort in our exile."

Boniface to Hwaetberht, Abbot of Monkwearmouth

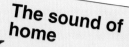

This gold cross was found in a church near Salzburg in Austria.

Requests sent abroad

"If there is any man in your diocese who can make vessels of glass well, will you send him to me when time is favourable, because we are ignorant and destitute of that art.

It would delight me also to have a harpist, for I have a harp and am without a player. I beg that you will not scorn my request, nor think it laughable."

Cuthbert to Lul

Presents sent home to England

"...a cloak, not of pure silk, but mixed with goat's wool, and a towel for drying your feet..."

Boniface to Daniel, Bishop of Winchester

"...some goat's hair bedclothes, as they are called here..."

Boniface to Hwaetberht

"...a multi-coloured coverlet to protect your body from the cold..."

Lul to Cuthbert, who turned it into an altarcloth

King Offa of Mercia

The larger, more powerful Anglo-Saxon kingdoms gradually took over the smaller ones. By the eighth century, Mercia had grown to become the most important kingdom south of the River Humber. Its most famous king was Offa, the first person to call himself 'King of the English'.

Offa's Dyke

Offa's Dyke stretches from sea to sea between England and Wales, and is nearly 238 kilometres long. It is made up of a ditch (about 2 metres deep) and an earth bank (about 8 metres high). There may also have had a stone wall running along the top in places. It must have taken a very long time to build.

It is not known whether Offa's Dyke was built as an act of peace, to mark an agreed border between the Welsh (the Britons in Wales) and the Anglo-Saxons, or whether Offa built it to stop the Welsh from invading Mercia. There had been regular wars between the Welsh and the Anglo-Saxons during the eighth century.

Trade

A remarkable letter to King Offa survives today. It was written by Charlemagne, the emperor of the western part of the Roman Empire. The letter tells us that the Anglo-Saxons were trading with the European mainland in the eighth century.

Charlemagne even sent a present along with the letter – a belt and an ancient sword.

Charlemagne asks Offa to send him some more woollen cloaks. He wants them to be the same size as they used to be. Perhaps the Anglo-Saxons had been trying to get away with using less wool.

In return, Charlemagne promises to send some 'black stones' to England. These were probably large stones from the River Rhine, used for grinding corn.

Coins

New silver coins appeared at the time of King Offa. They had Offa's name on them and were bigger than the old coins. This coinage is often called the 'first penny'.

Offa also issued a gold coin. He copied an Arabic gold dinar – but he put the writing on it the wrong way up!

Offa's queen, Cynethryth, issued coins in her own name too. She was the only Anglo-Saxon woman to do so. This is one of her coins.

The Vikings

The Vikings were the people of Denmark, Norway and Sweden who began to raid the coasts of Britain and Gaul in the eighth century. The first raid on Britain was in 793. The Vikings attacked the monastery at Lindisfarne and stole gold, silver and jewels to take back home with them.

The terror of the Viking raids is described by an Anglo-Saxon called Alcuin in a letter to the king of Northumbria. Here is part of the letter:

> ❝It is nearly 350 years that we and our fathers have inhabited this most lovely land, and never before has such terror appeared as we have now suffered from a pagan race.❞

Viking soldiers, wielding their swords and axes, can be seen on this gravestone from the monastery at Lindisfarne. It shows how closely the Anglo-Saxons associated the Vikings with death.

The Vikings raided the coasts of Britain because there was not enough good land at home for them to make a living. They carried off this beautiful book, decorated with gold and silver. An Anglo-Saxon couple called Alfred and Werburgh paid them some gold to give it back, and then wrote on the cover to say how they had saved it.

After the 860s, the Vikings stopped returning home after their raids and began to settle in England with their families. Within ten years, the Vikings had taken over all the kingdoms except Wessex. The *Anglo-Saxon Chronicle* gives a year-by-year account of how a large army from Denmark did this:

> 866: In this year came a great heathen army to England, and took winter-quarters from the East Anglians.
>
> 867: In this year the army went over the mouth of the Humber to York... and immense slaughter was made of the Northumbrians.
>
> 874: In this year the army went from Linsey [Lincoln] to Repton, and drove the king of the Mercians overseas.

The Anglo-Saxons called this army the 'Great Army' and they called these Vikings 'Danes'. But was the Great Army really as large and dangerous as the *Anglo-Saxon Chronicle* suggests?

Written evidence

The *Anglo-Saxon Chronicle* tells us that in the year 851, a Viking fleet of 350 ships came to the mouth of the River Thames to storm Canterbury. Even if there had been only ten men in each ship, that would still give a huge army of nearly 4000 men.

Archaeological evidence

There is now some archaeological evidence from Repton in Derbyshire, where the Great Army spent the winter of 874. It looks as if the Viking camp held an army of hundreds – not thousands – of men, and that as many people died from plague as from battle wounds.

A Viking sword

King Alfred of Wessex

By the year 875, Wessex was the only Anglo-Saxon kingdom still holding out against the Viking attacks. King Alfred defeated the Great Army in many battles and was able to build Wessex into a strong kingdom, where reading and writing were more important than war.

Alfred, however, nearly didn't survive the Viking attacks at all. When Guthrum, the leader of the Great Army, led the Danes in a surprise attack, Alfred was forced to hide in the marshes of Somerset. From here, he went on to defeat the Danes at the Battle of Edington in 878. The Great Army left Wessex, and Guthrum was converted to Christianity. Yet despite this victory, Alfred had to spend the rest of his life fighting the Vikings.

Father of the navy?

Alfred ordered ships to be built so that he could fight the Great Army at sea. The *Anglo-Saxon Chronicle* tells us what these ships looked like:

> 896: Then King Alfred ordered ships to be built to meet the Danish ships; they were almost twice as long as the others, some had 60 oars, some more; they were both swifter, steadier and with more freeboard than the others...

Archaeologists have not yet found any traces of Alfred's ships, so we do not know how well they measured up to this description.

Alfred was born at Wantage in Oxfordshire. This statue of him was presented to the town in 1877.

The English language

Before Alfred became King of Wessex, the few Anglo-Saxons who could read and write, such as Bede, wrote in Latin. It was Alfred who decided that all the young people in Wessex should learn to read – in English first, Latin could follow. He translated all the books he considered most important and sent copies of them around his kingdom, along with pointers for following the lines. The beautiful gold jewel in the picture below is the handle of a pointer. It has the words 'Alfred made me' round the edge.

Alfred also decided that a book should be written about everything that had happened to the Anglo-Saxons since their arrival in England. It was kept up to date like a diary and became known as the *Anglo-Saxon Chronicle*. A lot of our information about Anglo-Saxon England comes from this book.

Myths and legends

There are many stories told about King Alfred:

- he burnt some cakes whilst hiding in a peasant woman's home at Athelney, in the marshes of Somerset
- he disguised himself as a harpist to get into Guthrum's camp
- he invented the candle-clock as a way of telling the time

These stories were probably told about King Alfred because the person who wrote about his life needed some stories to tell!

A united kingdom

King Alfred's defeat of Guthrum at the Battle of Edington led to an agreement to divide England in two. The Vikings lived to the north of the old Roman road called Watling Street, in the 'Danelaw', and the Anglo-Saxons lived to the south. But Alfred, and the kings who came after him, did not intend the Vikings to rule this land for ever.

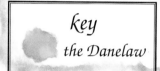

key
the Danelaw

Alfred's son, Edward the Elder, took the Danish part of Mercia from the Vikings, and Alfred's grandson, Athelstan, won back Northumbria. In 973, it was then possible for the next king, Edgar, to rule all of England. By destroying every kingdom except Wessex, the Vikings had helped to form the united kingdom of England.

Painting of King Edgar offering a book to Christ

Walled towns

Alfred knew it would be much easier to fight the Vikings from behind the walls of a town than on the battlefield. So he set about building high walls round the Anglo-Saxon towns. He also built 29 new towns. They had strong walls made of earth or stone.

The walled towns provided a safe place for the villagers to go to if they were attacked. You can see the remains of Alfred's walls in some towns today. Many other Anglo-Saxon towns, such as Hamwic, moved to new sites which were easier to defend.

Remains of the earth walls at Wareham in Dorset

Peace and good faith

Not all Anglo-Saxons and Vikings spent their time fighting one another. When the monks of Lindisfarne left their monastery under Viking attack in 875, they went to live on the mainland at Chester-le-Street. The Vikings who lived there gave them some land, and even swore peace and good faith over the body of Saint Cuthbert.

Place-names

Some places in England have kept the names of the pagan gods (see page 15), but most Anglo-Saxon place-names are more day to day:

burg, borough	= fortified place
den	= valley
ea, ey	= river
ham	= home
head	= hill
holt	= thick wood
ing	= people
ley	= clearing
mere	= lake
sted	= place
stow, stoke	= meeting place
tun	= farm
wald	= wood
worth	= fenced land

Viking names were added onto the map of Britain:

by	= village
thorpe	= small village

Although there was heavy Viking settlement in the North of England, the Anglo-Saxon names did not disappear. Many place-names are a mixture of both Anglo-Saxon and Viking.

Farming

By the tenth century, great changes were taking place not only in the towns but also in the countryside.

Iron tools

Anglo-Saxon farmers began to make a wider range of iron tools in the tenth century. The farmers in the above picture, taken from an Anglo-Saxon calendar of the farming year, are using scythes to cut their crops. Ploughs, forks, spades and axes were also made.

Farmers were able to grow more and more crops using these tools. With more food to feed everyone, people began to live longer. In the year 1066, there were about two million people living in England – twice as many as there had been 150 years earlier.

Hard work

This farmer had to plough the earth before the crops could be planted:

> ❛ I work hard. I go out at daybreak, driving the oxen to the fields, and I yolk them to the plough. However cold the winter is, I dare not stay at home for fear of my lord...every day I must plough a full acre or more. I have a boy driving the oxen with a goad-iron, who is hoarse with cold and shouting. And I do more also. I have to fill the oxen's bins with hay, water them and take out their litter... mighty hard work it is. ❜

What were these tools used for?

Landowners

In the seventh-century laws of King Ine of Wessex, Anglo-Saxon farmers were advised to put fences round their land to stop other people's cattle from damaging the crops.

By the tenth century, however, fences were no longer being put up and farming was taking place in large open fields. This change was brought about by the local landowner, who owned all the land in the village.

Archaeologists have found some of the estates, or manors, where the landowners lived. At Goltho, near Lincoln, the earlier Anglo-Saxon village was replaced by a very fine hall with a wooden fence round it. The picture below shows us what the manor would have looked like. Later on, in Norman times, it was turned into a small castle.

Changes in the climate

We hear a lot today about global warming, but changes in the climate have taken place throughout history.

When the Anglo-Saxons began to settle in England, they had to kill their cattle every November because they could not grow enough food in the winter to feed them. Their name for November was 'Blotmonath', or 'blood-month'.

In the tenth century, winters became shorter and milder and summers became longer and hotter. The Anglo-Saxons were now able to grow enough crops to keep their cattle throughout the winter. Farms grew in size and woodland had to be cut down to make more land for the cattle to graze on.

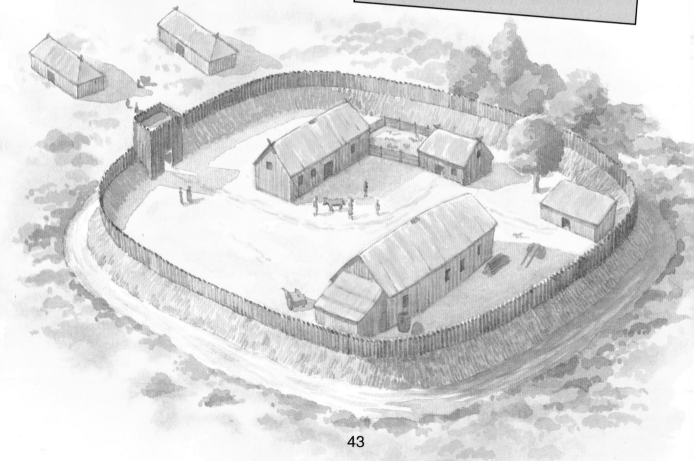

Maps, magic and medicine

The Anglo-Saxons drew a map of the world in the eleventh century, which was to stay the same for hundreds of years. However, there were still many things that they did not understand.

Medicine

Illness often led to death in Anglo-Saxon times and few people lived beyond the age of 40. Bede's *A History of the English Church and People* is full of miracle cures. Cuthbert, for example, is said to have suffered from a swollen knee that made him so lame he could not put his foot on the ground. Then an angel dressed in white rode up to him on a magnificently clothed horse and said, 'You must cook wheat flour with milk and anoint your knee with it while it is hot.' The cure is said to have worked.

This treatment seems no more unlikely than some other remedies found in Anglo-Saxon books.

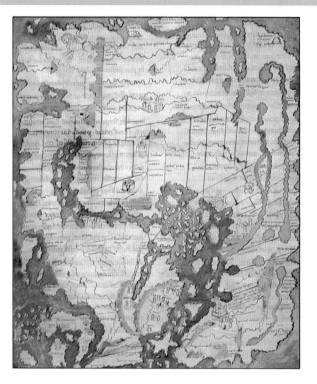

Toothache
'Take a leaf of holly and boil it. Lay the leaf in a saucer of water, raise the saucer to your mouth and yawn. The worms causing the toothache will come tumbling out.'

Madness
'If a man is a lunatic, take the skin of a porpoise [sea creature], work it into a whip, beat the man with it, soon he will be well.'

Snake bite
'Take a piece of wood from a tree from Paradise and lay it against the bite. The wood may be rather hard to find.'

Herbs were often used to heal wounds. This page is from a collection of herbal remedies. One remedy involved placing a paste made from nine herbs onto a wound, while reciting a charm into the patient's mouth and ears.

Astronomy

The Anglo-Saxon schools used Greek and Roman books to find out about the stars. They taught, wrongly, that the earth is at the centre of the universe and that the sun, moon and stars move round it. However, they also taught that the earth is round – not round like a shield, as Bede had said, but round like a ball.

The sky was thought to warn people of what was to come. Bede tells us that in the year 729, two comets appeared in the sky. They stayed there for nearly two weeks, striking terror into all who saw them. One comet moved across the sun as it rose in the east, while the other followed the sun as it set in the west. Bede thought this meant that there would be a disaster...and sure enough, an army of Arabs from the East attacked Gaul in the West, 'with cruel bloodshed'.

The picture below is part of the Bayeux Tapestry, a huge piece of embroidery made by English nuns in France in 1066. The embroidery tells the story of how William, Duke of Normandy, invaded England and defeated King Harold at the Battle of Hastings. This scene shows Halley's Comet, which appears in the sky every 76 years. You can also see Harold looking horrified on his throne.

1066 and all that

The last Anglo-Saxon king was killed at the Battle of Hastings in 1066, and William of Normandy became the first Norman king of England. However, the end of Anglo-Saxon England had started a long time before 1066.

The Danegeld

In the 980s, the Viking attacks on Britain started again. This time the Great Army from Denmark was determined to seize the kingdom of England.

The Anglo-Saxons decided to pay the Danes some money to get them to go away. This money became known as the 'Danegeld'. At first, the sum paid was £10 000. The Danes, however, kept on coming back and asking for more. Over the next 50 years, the English paid them £250 000.

King Cnut and Emma

In 1013, after twenty years of fighting, King Swein of Denmark finally seized the English throne from AEthelred. King Swein died soon after this and his son, Cnut, became King of England. We remember Cnut today in English folk-tales as King Canute, who tried to turn back the tide of the sea.

After AEthelred's death, King Cnut married his widow, Emma, who was a Norman princess. The Normans, like the Danes, were Vikings – but they had settled in Normandy in France.

Emma had the story of her life written down. Here she is receiving a copy of the book from the Norman monk who wrote it. Beside her are her two sons: the English Edward, who was the son of her first husband, AEthelred; and the Danish Harthacnut, who was the son of her second husband, Cnut.

King Harold

Edward became king after Cnut. He did not have any children and promised William, Duke of Normandy, that he would be the next king of England. But when Edward died in 1066, the English chose Harold, Earl of Wessex, instead. Edward was buried in the abbey he had built at Westminster in London.

Harold was not left to enjoy his kingdom for long. The Viking claim to the throne was now taken up by the Norwegians, who invaded England in September 1066. Harold marched north and defeated them at the Battle of Stamford Bridge. Almost immediately after this, he heard that the Normans had invaded Sussex. The effort of marching the length of the country and back again meant that the English army was exhausted by the time it reached Hastings.

The Battle of Hastings

The Battle of Hastings lasted all day and may only have been won by a trick William played on the English. He pretended to withdraw, but then turned and caught the English unprepared. Harold was killed in the battle and William became King of England.

Kings of England

978 –1013	*Æthelred* (English)
1013 –1014	*Swein* (Danish)
1016 –1035	*Cnut* (Danish)
1043 –1066	*Edward* (English)
1066	*Harold* (English)
1066 –1087	*William* (Norman)

Index

Answers: *page 13*
a baton used for weaving cloth
a key that was hung from a woman's girdle, or belt, round her gown
we don't know!

Published by BBC Educational Publishing, a division of BBC Enterprises Limited, Woodlands, 80 Wood Lane, London W12 0TT

First published 1992
© Rowena Loverance/BBC Enterprises Limited 1992
The moral right of the author has been asserted.

Paperback ISBN: 0 563 35001 6
Hardback ISBN: 0 563 35002 4

Colour reproduction by Daylight Colour, Singapore
Cover origination in England by Dot Gradations
Printed and bound by BPCC Hazell Books, Paulton

Acknowledgement is due to the following, whose permission is required for multiple reproduction:

PENGUIN BOOKS LTD for the extract from 'Beowulf'. Taken from *The Earliest English Poems* translated by Michael Alexander (Penguin Classics, second edition, 1977) © Michael Alexander, 1966, 1977

Photo credits Ancient Art and Architecture Collection **pp. 14 (bottom right), 22, 33**; Department of Antiquities, Ashmolean Museum, Oxford **p. 39**; Bodleian Library, Oxford **p. 6** *ms Canon Misc. 378, f. 154 verso*; The British Library **pp. 21** *ms Cotton Vespasian AI f. 30 verso*, **25** *ms Cotton Nero D. iv*, **40** *ms Cotton Vespasian A VIII f. 2 verso*, **42** *ms Cotton Tiberius BV f. 6 verso*, **44 (top)** *ms Cotton Tiberius BV Part 1 f. 56 verso*, **(bottom)** *ms Cotton Vitellius CIII f. 30*, **46** *ms Additional 33241, f . 1 verso - 2*; The British Museum **pp. 5 (top), 14 (top left), 15, 18, 19, 20, 28, 31, 35, cover**; University of Cambridge, Committee for Aerial Photography **pp. 9 (left), 11 (top)**; The Master and Fellows of Corpus Christi College, Cambridge **p. 23** *C.C.C..ms 173, f. 27 verso*; Archäologisches Landesmuseum der Christian-Albrechts-Universität **p. 5 (bottom)**; The Dean and Chapter of Durham **p. 27**; The Edinburgh Photographic Library **p. 17 (left)**; English Heritage **p. 9 (top right)**; Michael Holford **pp. 9 (bottom right), 17 (right), 45**; Kungliga biblioteket (the Royal Library) Stockholm **p. 36 (bottom)**; His Grace the Archbishop of Canterbury and the Trustees of Lambeth Palace Library **p. 26** *ms 200 f. 68 verso*; Lincolnshire County Council: City and Council Museum **p. 12**; Institute of Archaeology, University of Oxford **p. 14 (bottom left)**; Picturepoint Ltd. **pp. 7, 34, 38**; Axel Poignant Archive **p. 36 (top)**; The Repton Project/Malcolm Crowthers **p. 29**; St Edmundsbury Borough Council Museums Service **p. 11 (bottom)**; Sealand Aerial Photography **p. 41**; Sheffield City Museums **p. 14 (top right), 37**; Silkeborg Museum, Denmark **p. 4**; West Stow Anglo-Saxon Village Trust/St Edmundsbury Borough Council **p. 10**

Illustrations © David Price 1992 (pages 2–3, 6, 9, 11, 12–13, 15, 16, 18–19, 21, 22, 24, 28, 29, 30, 42 and *top* 47); © Tracy Fennell 1992 (pages 4, 27, 32, 35, 40 and *bottom* 47)